Instant Product Creation With Expert Interviews

Robert Plank
&
Thom Lancaster

By reading this document, you assume all risks associated with using the advice given below, with a full understanding that you, solely, are responsible for anything that may occur as a result of putting this information into action in any way, and regardless of your interpretation of the advice.

Printed in the United States of America

Dedicated to Internet Marketers everywhere, with thanks.

Instant Product Creation With Expert Interviews

Table of Contents

About The Authors

Robert Plank is a 26 year old home-owner from California. He is a full time Internet Marketer and PHP programmer.

To find out more about Robert, visit RobertPlankTraining.com.

Thom Lancaster is a UK based Internet Marketer. He has a particular interest in product creation.

To find out more about Thom, visit ThomLancaster.com.

Foreward

If you're an Internet Marketer, niche marketer or product creator, I don't need to tell you how useful interviews are.

When you carry out an interview with another person, you can make the recording and immediately have a product that's created for you.

It doesn't matter if you know next-to-nothing about the subject of the interview. You can still get a good interview out of the process.

In fact, that's one of the six interview techniques for instant product creation that expert Robert Plank shares for you here in this book, **Instant Product Creation With Expert Interviews**.

Robert has done literally hundreds of interviews, both of in the role of the interviewers, and in the opposite corner – being interviewed himself. So, he knows this area like no other.

Robert has also developed a really useful technique for solo product creation. He just carries out an interview where he plays both roles. That is, he comes up with a list of questions, ask himself those questions, answers them and has an instant product created ready to sell.

Once you master that technique, you'll never ever be short of a product to sell again.

I recommend that you take some time to devour this book carefully. Study the six different methods for interviewing other people. Choose which one of them works best for you. Then, simply get in contact with an appropriate expert and interview then.

Once you're familiar with that process, you can simply repeat in whenever you need a new product, or you want to enter a new niche.

It's that simple!

RobertPlankTraining.com

Best of luck with carrying out these interviews, and growing your product line through instant products.

Thom Lancaster
ThomLancaster.com

Chapter 1 – My Story

Hey, this is Robert Plank and in this book I'm going to show you how to create instant products by interviewing experts.

By the end, you're going to be ready to get crazy good at interviews.

Interviews, or not being able to do interviews, was a bottleneck for me for years and years. I always told myself that I would conquer that skill eventually or that I would find a joint venture partner who could go out and do interviews on my behalf or something, but I never got around to it. It was one step below learning how to record audio instructions. So it was really not a priority for me. I didn't think I could do it until I actually did it, and then it was like why haven't I been doing this for the past five years because it's super easy to do?

And here's why: Because you can make an instant product out of it. I could have taken all the information and typed it out and spent a whole day doing all this and getting all the things out that I wanted to say, but what I'm doing here is to bang out about 20 PowerPoint slides and just sit down in front of the computer. And I see one slide and I get my four bullet points, and I know exactly what I'm going to talk about and I just start talking.

That means it's a good way to make an instant product. You have 20 PowerPoint slides; you can squeeze between 20 minutes to an hour out of this. And I've been doing this over and over and over so it's very repeatable. I've done this so far to make, I think, about 30 videos for a membership site. So this is something you can use to put out a product very quickly, and you can do it over and over.

If you really were motivated and you had 30 really good subjects that you had a lot about, you could write each one on a calendar and make sure that at the beginning of each of those days that you would record an interview, either an interview with yourself or an interview of you talking to someone on that subject or them interviewing you.

Chapter 2 – Joint Venture Interviews

If you are trying to go the joint venture route with interviews, you try and approach people to get them to include your interview in their product as like a ride-along or as a bonus or something to get you more exposure. It's really easy to get people on board because so few people will do that. So few people actually have the guts to do a live call where someone else is recording it, where at any moment you could screw up and say the wrong thing, but you know what? I've screwed up on a lot of interviews and I've made stupid jokes about myself and I had awkward pauses, but you recover from that.

Maybe your first couple interviews you have really awkward pauses and you don't really recover, but eventually you do, but it still bugs you. But you just know that the recovering from the crash and burn moments are what you need to work on. So your next interview you'll keep focused on, "Yeah, I know there's going to be one or two awkward pauses in the half hour interview, but I'm going to be focused on how do I recover from that?" What happens when it takes longer? So maybe I get really panicked when I crash and burn, so I need to focus on staying calm. It's not the end of the world. Maybe you'll have one or two little subjects just written down on a piece of paper for emergencies, so if you really, really crash and burn you just go to one of these subjects.

You just figure out a way to solve these little problems and once you do you can really easily record your audios. You can really easily come up with a free CD so even like half an hour, I would consider that enough to stick on a free CD and then you will get people to pay you like $7 to ship this. That covers the cost of making this CD and shipping it. And then you promote your product. You talk for 20 minutes or somebody interviews you for 20 or 30 minutes about something, and then all through you have a call to action so people can listen to you an their computers, in their car, in their CD player while they're working, whatever. You're just being different than everyone else.

Or you could put this up on your blog or give it to your list as a nice bonus or make it as a bonus for one of your paid products or transform it into video.

Chapter 3 – Making Interviews Into Videos

Sometimes I'll take interviews, and I will make a PowerPoint slide for every single minute in the interview. So if the slide is 20 minutes I make a PowerPoint slide for each minute and then run through the PowerPoint, because you can arrange PowerPoints to automatically move forward after every 60 seconds. So you do that, record it in silence, and then dub the interview in as the audio in Camtasia when you produce the video – oh no – see, this I screwed up and now I'm recovering from it.

First, you take Camtasia and you record the PowerPoint and video playing all the way through in silence, and then later on when you produce it into a shareable video you just dub the audio right in; so that's the easy way to transform the audio into video. And even if you don't know how to do that you can always outsource it. And that's just one of many things you can do with audio.

And the idea is that even if you put out one audio product per month or one audio product every couple of weeks, you get a reputation as a guy who does interviews; especially if you're in a small niche; especially if you're in a non-internet marketing niche; you'll be the guy who does interviews. If everyone else is the exercise specialist or something or the exercise machine specialist – what home exercise equipment to get – and you're the guy who does all the interviews of all these home exercise equipment guys, you'll be the guy with all the contacts. And they'll know your voice, and they'll know your name, and you'll just be one step above everyone else.

Those are the reasons to record niche interviews because you can bang out products very quickly and over and over. It's easy to get people on board. You do a lot of different things with them and you get a lot of good contacts.

Chapter 4 – The Interview Mindset

It's not hard at all to record interviews because think about it. You hold regular conversations every day. I speak on the phone all the time with business associates who I just called them for five or ten minutes to ask them what they're doing today to keep them productive, and I'm telling them what I'm doing today to keep me productive, and we end up talking for like 30 minutes, 60 minutes.

And at the end of almost all these conversations I'm like, "You know what? We should have recorded that because that would have made an instant product." So you hold regular conversations every day and if they're with people in the same niche as you and they're with just not non-everyday people that you have in your life then they're – the other thing is you can monetize.

How many talk shows are out there where you have the host and then you have some actor or somebody come on and they just talk for 10 minutes, 20 minutes, and sometimes they've rehearsed but sometimes they don't; and sometimes what ends up on TV is way different from what they rehearsed. So you just have a conversation; just be a human. You've been on dates; you've had to hold down conversations for two or three hours sometimes; you've gone to job interviews, so you've had conversations where someone else was judging you, where it was really one-sided, where they might have been trying to trip you up or they might have been just trying to test your intelligence, and this is much easier than that.

If you've been on dates and you've had these long conversations, you've had conversations that lasted all night, this is way easier. If you've gone on job interviews where they've brought you back three or four times, and every time the guy was mean or was in a big group or was one-on-one in this really quiet room, and there were all these awkward silences, this is way easier because most of the time you're just fooling around; especially if you're in a niche that you really like and you're talking with someone that you know very well because you've worked with them over time, you've shared e-mails, you've promoted each other's stuff.

Those are the best kinds of interviews to have because you already know a little – all these little known tidbits about them and they know little tidbits about you, and you can just work things in.

Making an interview and doing an audio interview on your niche is a lot easier than all four of these things; I would say even easier than a regular conversation because regular conversations don't necessarily go anywhere. You haven't done any preparation and you don't know how long it's going to take, but with interviews you already have your set time limit or at least your goal for how long you want it to be at least.

Chapter 5 – Timing Interviews

Timing interviews is easy. Here's what you do.

You might say, "I want this to be at least 20 minutes but no longer than 30 minutes," and usually when I have an interview I'll have a countdown timer on my computer with the number of minutes left just so I don't go over, and I usually have maybe 3 to 5 questions if it's a niche

I'm kind of not sure of. And sometimes if it's a niche I really know, I'll just have the title of the interview, which I have phrased as a question just to make sure I don't get off topic.

And so this is a lot easier than regular conversations, easier than talk shows because you're not in front of a camera, you're not in front of hundreds of people, and you can just tune out the rest. So I've been on live teleseminar calls, and at first you're nervous but after like 30 seconds or a minute your brain just totally forgets that you're being broadcasted to all these people, and you just feel like it's a one-on-one with the person you're talking to. So all these things are much more difficult than having interviews. So your whole life has pretty much been practice for these interviews and doing more and more interviews is the only way you're going to get good at interviewing over time; because eventually all the skills, all the little, tiny things that you need to know to be a good interviewer that you didn't think about are going to become subconscious; they're going to become a part of you.

Chapter 6 – Finding People To Interview

If you do nothing else today find someone in your niche; it can even be someone you know. Maybe it's someone who's promoted for you as an affiliate and you want to interview them about what they did, what forums they marketed to, what ways did they upsell their niche product into your niche product.

Or maybe you just want to interview some random person, somebody you at least have a relationship with, somebody that has e-mailed you or commented on your blog or bought one of your products. Who knows? Just schedule an interview with them and the secret to this is you secretly plan to back out of it later.

So it's one thing to do the interview and then you're like, "Oh my god, I'm so scared. This is like a really big step," but if you schedule the interview and say, "I'll back out of it later," you're like, "OK, this is just a really simple exercise at making a little baby step towards getting into the interview process, but I plan to back out later." But the chances are that if you're the nervous, the shy kind of person, you'll be too nervous and shy to cancel so you'll end up doing the interview anyway. And you're going to be terrified a couple minutes before, but you do whatever you have to do to psych yourself up to get excited about doing this interview because you're both going to benefit from it and no one's going to laugh at you, no one's going to judge you. You're just going to have a conversation and you're going to keep it recorded so that you can – either one of you use it or you both use it or you make money from it or you give it away for free or you use it to build a list. You're making a product out of it, so relax.

Chapter 7 – Interview Layout

Enough feel good stuff. What's the layout of this going to be? I prefer to have my interviews go for about 20 minutes. 20 minutes is a good amount of time. It's around the average commute. If someone has the average commute from home to work, it's about 20 minutes. If they have a short commute then they can listen to the first half on the way to work; the second half on the way back. If someone's going jogging, if they're jogging a mile, say they're jogging two or three miles, they're jogging a couple of blocks around the neighborhood, this is a perfect length.

But if you get longer than 20 minutes then people are going to get bored or distracted, and if you get it any shorter then if they want to listen to a lot of the interviews you're not going to be able to go into enough depth and share enough information. So I prefer to have 20 minute interviews because they're really easy to break up if you want or put together. You can arrange them any way you want. If you want to have it longer than 20 minutes just hold multiple 20 minute interviews but try to make each one stand on its own. So if you want to tell people the three different subjects on building model trains and there's things you need to know as a beginner and as an intermediate person and as an advanced person. So first you hold the beginner's call and then you hold the intermediate call, but you don't want to reference anything in the beginner's call unless you totally have to.

Because you don't want to end up getting to say, "Hey, this is part 5 of the interview. Remember that thing from part 2 and the thing from part 4 and the thing from part 1?" You don't want to do that because people aren't always going to remember or they're going to listen out of order, and you don't want them to have to stop and skip around so you can make it work; you can say that you can listen to them in any order or if you want to listen to it in the correct order that's the best way to do it, but it's not required. You just don't want to do too much referring back to previous interviews. And just try to make each one stand out on its own.

Chapter 8 – The Technicalities Of Interviews

The technical details of carrying out interviews are - there's lots of ways to do them. I've heard of using teleseminar services and you both call in and record it but the few I've tried, they just give you really low quality recording with really low bit rate and it just wasn't worthwhile.

And there's people who recommend you go to Radio Shack and plug a thing into your phone and bring it to a tape recorder and connect that to your computer which seems like a lot of steps to me.

My favorite way does not require any special hardware other than the USB headset you should be using to record the audio. Other than that you just get Skype, which is a program that's been around for years and years and it's used – it's basically like a telephone system but for the internet. So you have people in your contact list, and you click on one of them; and then their phone starts to make ringing noises and they pick up; and then you can talk to them voice-to-voice as if it was a phone but it's over the internet.

You make sure the guy talking to you at least has a USB headset or some kind of a decent microphone, and you have a call going on Skype and use one of many Skype recording programs. My favorite is called Skype Recorder, and it will record the whole conversation into an .mp3 file and that's how you record the interview. And you preferably want to make it so that as soon as you start recording, that's the whole interview. So you don't want to have to edit stuff out later and say, "Don't worry that you said that. We'll edit it out." You want to try to get it right the first time.

Then, you call them. If they're at their computer call them on Skype for free or if they're not really good with the computer you can also use Skype to call a land line. It costs money, but it's really cheap. It's like 1 cent, 2 cents a minute or something. And so that'll be the same thing, you use Skype and a tape recorder and you can record the whole call. The difference is that you'll call their house or their cell phone and they'll pick up and their end will be from the phone, so it won't be as good as yours but it'll be OK.

After the call you want to normalize the sound file afterwards so that it's not quiet or loud on different ends because if you don't equalize – I don't know if the term is equalize or normalize or whatever – but if you don't do that your end will be really loud and the other end will be really quiet. So it'll be a pain for people to listen to because they'll have to turn the volume up real loud to hear the quiet guy and then it'll be blasting into their speakers. So that's kind of my pet peeve with listening to interviews is it's not normalized. So make sure that, using either GoldWave or using Camtasia, that you run – or I think Audacity will do it, too – you run the sound file through a normalizer so that the audio volume is the same.

Chapter 9 – The Note Taking Strategy

When you take the interview, here's how to take notes. I take a blank 8½ x 11 sheet of paper just off of the printer, not lined; this isn't school; I'm not trying to take notes; we're just talking. And if somebody says something really interesting that I didn't know before that I kind of want to explore, I just jot it down really quick. I don't want to make huge, proper notes because I want to be focusing on what they're saying and not what I'm writing, so I don't want them to distract me for too long.

I just write down a sentence or two.

Or if something's confusing and I want them to explain it more, I'll write that down. But two-thirds of this will be totally useless. So if something's important I'll make sure to circle it or box it or write a number in a circle next to it just so I know that's a point I want to hit on, if not for them to clarify something but at least at the end when I summarize everything. So jot stuff down; make notes; make notes on the left, on the right. You don't have to go in any order; just make sure it makes sense to you.

You're writing these notes down. The main reason is so at the end you can tie at most three or four ideas together to give your listeners like a to-do list or some kind of action plan, you know, "Go out and do this now that you've got this information." And the secondary reason is to backtrack, so if they skipped over something that was really interesting or really confusing you can hit them on that. But don't go further than 30 or 60 seconds back because I don't know if you've had conversations with people like this in your life. I haven't very often but every once in a while it just gets me where you talk about one subject – so say you're talking about model trains and you're talking about the wheels on model trains. You talk about what are the best size and the best thickness and how much grease to apply or whatever and then you get talking about train tracks and that's good, too. And then you talk about what kind of light should be on the front of the train, and then he starts talking about the wheels again. He keeps dragging you back to the beginning of the conversation and makes no progress, so you don't want to be that guy. You don't want to be the guy who asks about the wheels five minutes after that part of the conversation was over.

So if you jot down notes and you want somebody to clarify something, jump in and if you have to interrupt them a little bit, do it. But you don't want to – if you've waited longer than 30 to 60 seconds it's too late. So only backtrack these questions 30 to 60 seconds back.

Chapter 10 – The Six Types Of Interviews

Now that you know the technical stuff, you know the structure and how to take the notes to give the best interview possible, let's go over what kind of interview you'll be giving. Of the interviews I've done I prefer these six different types of interviews. So if I'm going to do an interview and I have the topic, I need to think of a hook. I need to think of something really interesting because you don't want to just say, "Let's talk about model trains." And usually if you are you have one of these six items in mind.

So these are the six.

The first is the most basic. It's the scripted interview, and this is where you have questions. So maybe you'll have five questions or ten questions about model trains, and you'll just say, "OK, what kind of wheels should I have for model trains?" and the other guy will talk and hopefully he's a good talker. So the scripted interview is good if the other guy is a good talker because this is where you're a total newbie; you don't know what you're doing and hopefully he'll talk and then after he talks to you all about the wheels say, "OK, now what about the sides of the train? What kind of sides should I have on my model train," and he'll talk and talk and talk.

These are the kinds of interviews where you just need to do it to get experience. If you can't do any of these other types, if you're scared of having the awkward silence or saying the wrong thing or not knowing what to say, this guarantees that you always know what to say because you'll always have these questions, but it's also the worst kind of interview and we'll get to that in a little bit.

The next step up from that is where you're interviewing an expert but you are a newbie. I call this the game show host. The game show host, like Bob Barker – The Price is Right, Regis Philbin – Who Wants to Be a Millionaire, they'll ask you stuff like, "What city are you from? How old are you? How many kids you have?" They'll ask the stupid questions. He knows nothing about you; you're a total stranger. So this is good if you have no relationship with the person, and you're a total newbie on the niche and you just say, "I'm dumb, so please be slow and please make it simple for me. And I might have dumb questions but I'm warning you beforehand."

You're not going to go in and pretend to be an expert and pretend to know everything he has to say. You're dumb,

OK? You're being the dumb person, which this type of interview has the most appeal.

Then you've got this Stu McLaren, I call it, interview where you're both experts. I used to try a few different types of interview styles, but then this guy interviewed me and he was really, really good, so he went in and I was kind of mean. I didn't tell him what the topic was he was going to be interviewing about and he asked all the right questions and he talked to me for 20 minutes and got info out of me for 20 minutes. And he interviewed like 15 people that night, I think, all in a row, so he's really good at interviewing.

And so his technique is where you're both experts and you know the right questions to ask. If you're the one giving the interview, you don't really talk a lot and you pretty much ask the same two or three questions over and over, which I'll get to, but this is the kind of interview where you don't need a lot of preparation. You just need to listen really well and take decent notes that at the end you can recap everything they said. But this is the kind of interview where you're both experts and you know that the other guy has a lot of info and all you have to do is push the right buttons and it'll just come to you.

And you've got the challenge interview, so this is where you're not just getting information; you're not just getting tips; you're saying, "What can I do with these tips?" Or how would you do this thing that you're an expert in in X number of days? So you could say, "If you knew nothing about model railroads and you only had $20, how would you complete a full railroad set in 7 days or less?" because it's 7 days before Christmas, and you want to have this whole model railroad set for your kid built by Christmas. So how would you complete that task in that number of days.

Then you could do the how-you-did-it kind of interview, so you just interview someone about what's their story and what did they do to get to where they are now. If you're interviewing a guy about model railroad trains and you say, "How many different kinds of model railroad trains do you have?" And he says, "120." And you say, "OK, well tell me about your first model railroad train set? And how old were you? And how much did it cost you? And did you put it together or was it already made? Was it the right kind of model train to get? And then what was your second model train and how did you get from that very first model train to where you are now with the 120 model trains? And what three or four things did you learn along the way?"

And then the final kind of interview, which I'm not normally good at but I'm trying to do more of, is the back-and-forth, where you're having more of a discussion in the interview. This works better if someone's interviewing you, so they're asking all these questions and every once in a while you kind of turn it around on them. So if you're both experts on model trains and the guy says, "Well, which kind of model trains do you like? Do you like the huge ones or the little tiny ones?" And you can say, "Well, when I was younger I liked the little tiny ones because I had really good eyesight. And the small ones I'd link a bunch of cars together and have the switch track and it was really complicated. And I had a little model trees and all these decorations, but now that I'm older I have a bigger house and I prefer to have the bigger trains. And I can't see as well these days, so doing the small stuff wouldn't really work, but what's your take on that?"

So you answer the question but you be nice to the guy and you turn it around on them and ask for his opinion. And also, if he's not very responsive you say, "Do you agree with me or do you disagree with me?" And if it still doesn't help say something outrageous like," I think the small ones are stupid. The big trains are the best. Don't you think?" And maybe he's a pushover and he'll go along with it or if you know he's a guy who has real strong opinions and maybe he'll disagree and you can have a real nice emotional interview going on.

Those are the six types, and in the next chapter I'll go through each one for you.

Chapter 11 – The Scripted Interview

Here's how you approach the scripted interview.

This is the interview where you just read your questions one at a time, let them answer. You don't really deviate from the questions; don't do a lot of impromptu stuff. You just ask the question; he answers; and you ask the next question.

And then at the end you give a 60 second summary.

At the end you talk for a minute about what the answers were so that for people skimming they can get the really concise version. And this is good if you're nervous or a newbie because I knew a guy who tried to start a membership site, and it was basically like 10 bucks a month, I think. And every month there would be a new interview with an expert on the subject in his niche. Till this day he won't let me listen to the audio because it was so bad. He was like, "OK, first question: What do you think about this?" And the guy he was interviewing was really good at answering questions because he had interviewing experience before and he would be real nice and be like, “Oh yeah, you know, here’s my answer,” and he’d talk for like 5 minutes.

And then the guy giving the interview was super nervous and he’d be like ”OK, good. Next question” and the next question would be on a totally different subject. So he was pretty much like a robot just asking the questions, and there’s nothing wrong with that. It’s not going to be the best interview in the world, but it’s better than nothing. And so it’s good if you’re nervous but it’s bad if you want really good interviews. So you’re not going to have a lot of the interaction, just a simple “answer my questions.”

If you're not sure which one to start with just try this one, and if that one doesn't work then go with the game show host interview, and if that one doesn't work go with the Stu McLaren interview. So even if you failed six times, you have six interviews. So no matter what, even if you screw up the interview somewhere along the way, don't stop the interview. Just like, I'm not stopping right now. If I have mistakes I keep going. I say I'm not going to totally stop this; I'm going to keep going. And that's what you have to do with the interviews sometimes. You'll screw up but you have to keep going.

Chapter 12 – The Game Show Host Interview

The next type of interview is the "I am a newbie" or the game show host interview. And this is where you don't know anything about the subject, so you say," I'm a total newbie. I'm dumb, so please be slow. Just tell me the three things I need to know about ____."

Say, you're interviewing a guy about breeding snakes. So how to find the two correct species of snakes and put them together or however it's done and put the egg in an incubator after it lays the egg so that you can get the snakes with the all-white, the albinos with the funny patterns, or the ones that are worth thousands of dollars, so you say, "I don't know anything there is about snake breeding. Tell me what are the three things you need to know about snake breeding?" So maybe you could ask, "How do I do it? Like what's the process? How do I get my first snake or my first embryo or egg or my breeding kit or however it's done and where do I go for advice? So what types of forums should I look at and which types should I stay away from?"

You're doing this interview to save time, save all this frustration, maybe weeks or months of time trying to figure out, "OK, this forum doesn't work. There's all that time wasted. I need to go to this forum." So give me the three basic things I need to know as a beginner. And you might want to do ten minutes of research on Google or Wikipedia just to get the basics, just so you can understand things like what's a Punnett square and how do I, if I have this color snake and that color snake, how do I know what kind of snake I'll end up with.

It's just so you're not a complete newbie, but you can still be ignorant. The whole theme of this interview is going to be that you're ignorant and that's going to be the appeal because you can market this to other people who are ignorant, who know nothing about breeding snakes, who want to start doing it the same way you're doing it. So this is good if you want the widest possible audience; if you want lots of beginners.

Then you could do more interviews later on more advanced subjects, but just not the "I'm a newbie" interview. So this is bad if you want multiple interviews with the same person because you can only pretty much do this once or twice. He can only educate you on so many basics before you're going to have to start moving up to a higher level. So this is good to get started. This is good if you've tried the scripted interview and either you got bored with it or you just didn't like the results or you wanted to try something else.

Chapter 13 – The 'We're Both Experts' Interview

If you are an expert, so you're not a newbie and you're not afraid of trying a little bit of conversation do the "we're both experts" interview. This requires no preparation and no structure. All you need to do is just get an interview topic. So to do that I'll either think of them myself, so a problem I'm personally having, or if I want something really good I'll ask my mailing list to get interview topics. And I'll have between 30 and 100 people reply and the majority of that stuff will be the same question over and over if you just group them into categories. So I'll say there's my question. There's the biggest pain point that people have, the thing that causes them the most anger, the most frustration, their bottleneck; and now I know what to ask about.

If you had a mailing list about breeding snakes your bottleneck could be why do my snake eggs keep dying before they're even hatched? So then you can ask that to your snake breeding expert, and I'm sure that from there you can go on and on on different tangents about what possible things could be wrong and what things to try. So it could be like the climate; it could be the incubator machine; it could be the time of year or the species you're trying to breed. Who knows?

And also with this kind of interview it helps if you do a background check, I like to call it, on the person who you're interviewing. So this doesn't mean literally call the FBI or look up their police record. It means if they have a website look at it and figure out what they do. So what specifically in their niche do they do? What specifically about snake breeding do they do? Do they just sell the incubator machines or do they sell the actual snakes?

If they post on forums what subjects do they talk about? What subjects do they write the most about? Or what gets them the most excited? What's their latest blog post? What's their latest product they launched? So you just want to get a couple of ideas on possible directions the interview could go. And those are also if you have the pauses, the awkward silences, you have a new idea to hit them with.

When I was interviewed by this guy, Stu McLaren, the nicest guy on the internet, he was the freaking best person who has interviewed me ever. He knew a couple things about me from my blog, so he asked that one question to get me going and I answered it; I talked for a couple minutes. And he goes, "Well, this one little thing you mentioned in your first answer, let's explore that. Let's go deeper into that. So tell me a more about this." And then we did that, and then he would say, "All right, moving along what's the next thing?" And then we talked about that and he said," OK, let's explore that. Let's go deeper."

He would just keep every answer, would move along to the next thing to the next thing to the next thing and every time I mentioned some key word – so the questions were like what did I do differently in 2008. Or how did I get started or something like that, so then I would say things like, "Well, first I did freelancing. Then I started building mailing lists. Then I started doing actual product launches. Then I started doing video." And then I said, "At this point I had a day job," and he'd say, "OK, let's explore that. How do you balance a day job with internet marketing?"

And we'd explore that and then he'd start kind of winding down so near the end he would give me the easier questions. And then he gave me two chances to give me the final thought. So a couple minutes away he's like, "What's the best _____? So what's the best thing out of all these things you mentioned that you did in the last couple of years or in 2008?" And I'd say, "OK, this, for these reasons." And he's like, "All right, as we're winding down do you have any absolute final thought to say to our listeners? What should they take away from this? What should they do immediately after listening to this interview?"

That's the format we would take. He would just do four "let's explore that's" and two final thoughts. So the first final thought would be, "Out of what you said what's the best thing or what's the best thing period, maybe not even including the things you just said" and then the last thing was the final thought, the takeaway. And that interview lasted for 20 minutes.

Chapter 14 – The Challenge Interview

You could do the challenge interview, so this is – it's kind of a combination of the newbie and the expert. So it assumes that you have some knowledge but you're acting like a newbie. So you say, "Based on what expertise you have in snake breeding how would you breed your first snake egg in two months, in 60 days?" Or how would you, based on your expertise in landing a job interview, how would you get a job in 14 days if you had no references, no resume, and we were in a recession, and nobody in town was hiring? Or if you were an eBay expert, how would you make a hundred dollars in 24 hours? Or if you were a weight loss expert, how would you lose 10 pounds in 30 days?

But the secret to this is it has to match their expertise, so it has to match the thing they're the best at and that no one else is better at. And if that means you have to get super specific, so if you have to say if you were going to lose 10 pounds in 30 days by swimming, how would you do it? So if they're the swimming weight loss expert then that's what you'd do. But this works really well if they're the best or one of the best authorities on something very specific. They have to be an expert on the subject but it's bad if no one's prepared.

So this is the kind of thing where maybe you want to warn them a day or two in advance. And say, "Look I'm going to ask you about how would you do this in this number of days. How would you get a job in 14 days, so could you just write down three or four little points about what would you do on day one or on the first week, and what would you do on the second week" just so they're not going into it blind. Because I've just found with the challenge interviews you can do it without any preparation, but it's just a little bit sloppy. And you're always going to think of stuff after the interview that you wish you had thought of, so it works better with a little bit of preparation.

Chapter 15 – The Biography Interview

The next interview is the biography interview, the how-you-did-it, how they got from there to here. So you can say, "How long have you been breeding snakes?" And they say, "Five years." They say, "From 2005 to 2010," and you say, "OK, what did you do in 2005 for the whole year? What did you do?" And he's like, "Well I've been reading on snakes for a few years before that, and I bought this book and I've bought that book, and I have a friend who had snakes and I was always kind of jealous so in 2005 I bought my first snake, but I got a glass cage that was way too big and he died. He didn't last very long. And then I bought a different size cage for the right size of snake because I actually did research, but the temperature was wrong, and he died."

You just ask them about the first year, the second year, the third year, or maybe the first couple years or maybe the first couple months, whatever applies, whatever timeline you're trying to keep track of, just ask them about specific years because I've found that if you ask them about certain time periods they'll be a lot more specific and they'll give you a lot better nuggets of information that you can explore.

The most important thing is you keep track of what changed, both good and bad. So instead of him telling some long story about buying this snake and buying that snake and this type and that type you get him to say things like, "I bought the big tank or the little tank," or "I researched it and finally got the right tank instead of guessing." So you keep track of what changed both good and bad, especially the bad because the mistakes are more entertaining than the successes. Everybody loves a guy who fails. I mean think about Donald Trump. He declared bankruptcy and then he became a super rich dude doing all this real estate stuff, mostly from reality shows.

But anyway people just love the guy who fails and fails and then succeeds because they're learning about your failures instead of experiencing them themselves, and they save a lot of time. So that's the how-you-did-it interview, and it's really easy to crank out like ten of these. And they'll be super boring so just keep the how-you-did-it to one or two interviews per person because otherwise it's going to be boring to have, "OK, here's the 2005 interview and here's the 2006 and here's the 2007." Unless you have a lot of really interesting, crazy stuff in there, it's going to be really boring. So I wouldn't do a lot of these but if you're just stuck about what to interview someone, you have no idea whatsoever, just do the how-you-did-it interview, and that's probably what most interviewers would think of if they didn't know about these different types and they would interview somebody this is probably what they would go to, the how you did whatever it is you did that makes you an expert.

Chapter 16 – The Back-And-Forth Interview

Then you've got the back-and-forth interview. This is kind of like the expert interview, but somebody asks you questions and then you answer. And most of the time you'll just answer and then he'll move you on to the next thing but a lot of the times – I've been playing with this recently – you turn it around and you say, "What do you think about this?"

So if you both know a lot about snake breeding and he asks you – and especially this works well with opinions, so he's like, "What's your favorite breed of snake to breed?" And you can say, "Oh, bull pythons are my favorite. What about you?" And that way it becomes more of a discussion, more of an eavesdropping thing, but it's important not to flip it around and make it about you. So you don't want to be interviewing someone and then he asks your opinion and then you totally take over and you talk for five or ten minutes because I've been interviewed like that. I've been interviewed where I was supposed to be the one giving the answers, and suddenly he's talking more than me.

This is good if you both have overlapping skill sets. You can kind of do a really good back-and-forth, do a good cop/bad cop, Abbott and Costello type of thing, but bad if you're not good at interviews yet because you're going to do this thing where one guy takes over and you don't want that. So an advanced interview technique if you've already got the hang of the first five interviews; I just threw this one in for you; you can graduate up to the back-and-forth interview, and it's a lot of fun, believe me.

Chapter 17 – It's Okay To Suck

As we're coming to the end of this book now, I think it's fair to share something with you.

I know that your first few interviews are going to suck. Mine did. I'm sure most people in the world's interviews sucked. They just had a lot of practice. So you're going to want to overcome one obstacle at a time. So maybe you'll interview, and you'll listen to your interviews later or you'll ask the guy you interviewed what he thought, and you'll notice that you asked a lot of unclear questions or your speaking was unclear, like your language itself or you slurred your words, spoke too fast or too slowly. There was just one thing to work on.

Maybe there were a lot of things wrong, but you have one thing to work on which is whatever your biggest problem is. Maybe you're talking too much so you're the guy who's supposed to be asking the questions, and you're talking more than the guy answering. Or you're talking too little so you don't ask enough questions, and the guy answering has to make up for it or vice versa. So maybe you're being interviewed and the guy has all these questions to ask, and he asks you one question and you go off on a tangent the whole time and he never has a chance to ask anything else.

Or maybe you are being interviewed and you don't talk enough and there's all this silence so he keeps having to scramble to come up with more questions because you didn't answer him all the way. Or maybe pausing too often or not enough. So you just quickly jump from thing to thing; there's no transition and no one wants not enough pausing. People like to be relaxed when they listen to stuff. But they don't want to be put to sleep either, so you don't want to pause for 30 seconds or for a whole minute. See that? That's just too weird. That's eerie. That's awkward and that's creepy, so normal conversations don't last with these long pauses. So it's okay to pause for a second, but just don't pause for like 30 seconds.

And conversation backtracking. So this is the thing where the guy is talking about the wheels of the train, which do not go round and round. He's talking about the wheels of the train five minutes ago and then you go back and start talking about the wheels of the train again. The conversation has to move forward and then you can work on conversation tangents, where you're talking about one thing and you go off on some other subject that's totally unrelated. And so these are just the things you're going to want to overcome with your interviewing. Think about one and focus on that one thing and just keep that in mind in the back of your head when you're doing interviews. Don't be thinking about it all the time; just be aware of it and after you conquer that you can conquer the next thing.

Chapter 18 – Summary

Let's review the six different types of interviews we went over. With the scripted interview where I have these set of questions; the game show host where I'm a total newbie, the Stu McLaren interview where you just say you understand what he's saying and then he mentions one thing and you say, "Well, can we explore this?" And then he mentions this thing and you say, "Can we explore this?" And then you do that four times for a 20 minute interview. At the end you say, "Out of what you just said, what's the best?" And then, "What are your final takeaway thoughts?"

Then you've got the challenge where you say, "How would you accomplish this task, which you're an expert in, in this number of days or this number of hours or this number of months? So how would you quit your job and retire in three months or less?" Or the how-you-did-it. So if you're interviewing Donald Trump and you could say, "How did you get from having nothing to building up this real estate empire?" And then "What happened to cause you to become bankrupt and then how did you build it all up again? So what's your story?"

Or you can have the back-and-forth. So this is where you're an expert on remote control airplanes and the guy interviewing you is an expert on remote control airplanes and he asks you, "What's your favorite kind of remote control airplane?" And so you give your opinion on that and you turn it around and say, "Well, now that I've shared, really quick, what's your favorite kind of model airplane?"

RobertPlankTraining.com

Chapter 19 – Last Minute Advice

Some last minute advice for you. You don't have to be an expert on everything. You don't have to necessarily be an expert to give an interview. Don't be afraid to say "I don't know."

That was probably the best advice I was given for a real world job interview because so many people can detect crap. They can detect when you're trying to fool them or trying to get around a question. If you don't know something just say "I don't know." Just say, "That is not my area of expertise." And so you don't have to be an expert. If you're asking the questions, you definitely don't have to be an expert and you can play that up. But if you're answering the questions you can say, "I'm not an expert on this and here's why." So instead of trying to avoid the question you get it out of the way really quickly that you don't know and you make it a non-issue.

A couple last things. If you're interviewing someone else, just remember they're on the spot. The focus is on them to deliver answers, not you. So relax. And if you're being interviewed just be aware that yeah you're on the spot, but you're the expert and you can probably answer any question they throw at you and they're not going to try to trip you up; they're not going try to lure you. This isn't court; they're not going to try to sabotage this. This isn't some scary job interview. They want a good interview just as much as you do so they're not going to sabotage it, and they'll probably help you along. If you screw up, they'll probably do something to help you out and to help you recover. So don't worry about it.

RobertPlankTraining.com

Chapter 20 – Conclusions

Thanks for reading **Instant Product Creation With Expert Interviews**.

Here's your one goal for today. It's to talk to somebody you email or talk to on the phone or joint venture with or have some kind of business dealings with in the same niche. Schedule an interview with them and then go back and cancel later because you're probably not going to cancel.

In no time at all, you'll be crazy good at interviews!

Robert Plank
RobertPlankTraining.com

www.ingramcontent.com/pod-product-compliance
Lightning Source LLC
Chambersburg PA
CBHW030008190526
45157CB00014B/1233

* 9 7 8 1 4 6 1 1 1 5 7 7 9 *